HURT UNSPOKEN

WRITTEN BY:

CARLA L. DENNIS

This book is dedicated to every man, woman, boy, or girl that has ever been sexually violated. For many, they will carry what happened to them to their grave. I, on the other hand, was prompted over a year ago to write this book. What you will read in the pages to follow is my truth, my past. This part of my life is something that I chose to never share with anyone. Up until now, I kept it buried deep- oh so very deep, in the innermost bowels of my being. I suppose that I never would have spoken about it had I not personally experienced and seen how this type of crime has the potential to ruin someone's life if not properly dealt with. So, I write… not to bash anyone, not for acclaim, not to be anything or anyone other than who I am, not for pity, and not to convince anyone to change their mind about what they think transpired. I write for my own personal liberation and for those whose voices may never be heard. People need to understand that when a person is sexually assaulted, it DOES impact their life in a major, negative way. It did mine.

Hear my heart in this. To put this experience- this life altering experience, on paper was the best way for me, personally, to get it out. And while I take the covers off what, even now, makes me uncomfortable to speak about, I am going to take this time to heal. Now that I can deal with this from an adult perspective, I am going to allow myself the time and space to recover properly. While I am not bitter or angry, some things that I say may come across as that. I am sure that as I write, I will feel a plethora of emotions. Grant me that. After all, you are reading about MY experience. I won't minimize what took place to make someone else feel good about themselves, neither will I alter my truth. I will, however, take you through a timeline of events that are all related to this one horrific incident.

My prayer for this book is that it gets into the hands of people that really need it. Oftentimes, people that have been sexually assaulted are *grossly* misunderstood. Cries for help get misconstrued. Those cries sometimes manifest in promiscuity (for me it did), rebellious behavior, intentional obesity (so as to not appear attractive), and even silence. Unfortunately, this is not an exhaustive list. There's way more. Don't be so quick to write someone who's gone through this off. You don't know their day to day struggle just to stay atop the demons in their mind.

There are several people who have been instrumental in the writing of this book. But first, I must thank God. Lord, you have been with me through it all! The shame, guilt, fear... everything! The ways that you made for this book to come to pass, only YOU get the glory for it. To EVERY person that contributed to this project- you, God, and I know who you are. I THANK YOU! Your willingness to share your experiences, and to sincerely lend a hand has not gone unnoticed. Watch and be amazed at what God will accomplish through our concerted efforts. I give to you: Hurt Unspoken.

I was raped. There, I said it. Before it happened to me, I had my own opinion about what rape was. While I had heard very little about it, I knew very little about it. Most fifteen year olds, I would venture to say, probably are not thinking about something like that. But, it happened… to me. My life would be forever changed.

I was fifteen years old, and I had this watch that I adored. It was a Swiss made watch- which at the time was a big deal. My watch was white, black, and red, and I absolutely loved that watch! Here's how it began: my watch was taken away from me, I wanted it back, and I was going to get it back…plain and simple. I'll call the two people that were involved Y and Z (the identity of the two males will not be revealed). I walked down the driveway, around the corner into the basement of Z's house- which from the outside seemed non-threatening. That is where and when the nightmare began.

To me, it was irritating- them taking my watch, but I didn't look at *them* as a threat. I went to school with them. One of them (Y) I had considered my 'boyfriend'. So, to answer your question: "Well, why did you go in the basement?", this would be why. I didn't have my guard up with them because they were my classmates. I knew them from our neighborhood. We caught the same bus to school for Heaven's sake! To me, there was absolutely no reason to feel that something was about to go down.

Some things did go down. And no matter how many times I pleaded with them not to do the unthinkable, their minds were made up. My pants were taken away from me- the one who lived at the house took them upstairs, and they proceeded to rape me. At one point, the sister of Z came home. I don't recall what the exact threat was word for word, but I was threatened. I believed them, so I didn't bring any attention to myself. I didn't scream, try to get away, knock anything over, nothing. Man, do I wish I had done something incredibly courageous, something crazy… something!!! Then, just maybe the outcome would have been different. Maybe the outcome would have been different for all of us- me and my family, as well as for them and their families.

You know something? And, yes, I am going a little off the trail here. But, to me it seems that this type of crime is all about control- mind control, body control, just all out control. And for someone that is like how I used to be, they could wind up as easy prey. Call it stupidity, or whatever you may, but I just did not believe that they were even capable of doing what they did. For one, it just didn't make any sense. I hadn't provoked them to make them want to do me any harm- at least not in my eyes. I didn't have on any provocative clothing, or any of the other number of reasons that people give to justify why people sexually assault other people. There was absolutely NO reason for them to do what they did.

As I type, I remember their sinister laughs and grins. I was like their rag doll, and they did what they wanted to do to me. There is absolutely no other thing that I have experienced in my life that I can compare to what happened on that day- or the aftermath. Nothing. I mean NO THING! This one incident significantly changed the course of my life afterwards.

After I was 'released' from the basement and given my watch, I went straight home. I lived only 5-10 minutes away from where this happened. I told my mother what happened, and she called the authorities. I remember the officer being very compassionate. He took me down to the station in his patrol car. I rode in the front seat, and I remember just an overwhelming feeling of exhaustion. There were several officers that questioned me for what seemed like forever in this room at the police station. They seemed to have been angered, concerned, and whatever else one might feel in a situation such as the one I found myself in. I remember them offering me something to eat- I had no appetite. I was given a Sprite. Maybe they felt as if this would somehow make me feel better.

From there, I remember going to the hospital. The hospital employee asked me a lot of questions about what had happened. I'm guessing this was some type of mental assessment. And then, there was the physical assessment. I couldn't stand for the doctor to do anything more than just look at my private area, so that part didn't take very long. I was given a pill that would keep me from becoming pregnant- and I thank God for that. I know that there are women that have been raped, only to find out later that they were pregnant. It brings tears to my eyes to even think about how that must feel. Only the love of God can give a woman the wherewithal to raise a child out of such a violating act. I am beyond grateful that I did not have to raise one of their children!

This happened on a Friday, after school. I decided to go back to school the following Monday, and act as if it had never happened.

Have you ever heard people in church say something to the effect of going from "glory to glory"? Well, it was like that for me, only the opposite of glory. I went from one bad situation to the next, to the next, and then on to the next. I got on the bus, and I quietly took my seat- something I normally did. There was this ugly, black (black as in very dark skinned) boy who was always, ALWAYS rude to me. As I think back on it, he was like a demon from hell. He made this one remark that went something like: "She got double hand cuffs over the weekend". I didn't say anything, I just sat there in silence. How he knew, I don't know. For that matter, how did anyone outside of me, my family, the police, and the others involved find out about what happened? Now, maybe I am giving humanity too much of the benefit of a doubt, but who in their right mind brags about raping someone? I mean, I am pretty sure that this type of thing does happen, but WHY?!?! This is the only reason that I can think of that would explain how people found out about this. I doubt if someone, just on a whim, went to the courthouse to view public records, and came across my case against Y and Z. That was highly unlikely. But, however they found out, people knew. I recall as I was walking through the gym to the locker room, this one guy says to me: "Y and

Z finally found their home (jail), huh?" This guy- bless his sweet heart and silly head, had pure intentions I suppose. It didn't make me feel one ounce better.

I recall sitting in my Literature class. I caught my teacher staring at me. To this day, I still remember the look that was on her face. It was as if she wanted to just come over and pick me up, and make all of the bad go away. There was such compassion in her eyes. She didn't say anything to me about what happened, but I was relieved knowing that she was not against me.

I was in Spanish class, and my instructor referred to the incident. There was no compassion there. To this day, I somewhat have a feeling that she knew that the 'young lady' involved was me. Like a dummy, to minimize the blow- as well as try to deflect my classmate's attention, I smiled as if she wasn't referring to me. I tried to act as if I had nothing to do with what happened. On the inside, I was so very embarrassed, hurt, and humiliated. If it were possible, I would have turned beet red from my head to my toes from the embarrassment. Yet, as I, on the outside, tried to make it appear as if I had shaken it off, in silence I trudged on.

The house that I grew up in had a deck built onto the back of it. Normally visitors went to the front door and knocked, or rang the doorbell. But on this day, there was a knock at the back door. If I remember correctly, my mom opened the door. It was the brother of Y. My parents did not tell me what the conversation was about, and neither did I ask. Years later I found out that he came by to try and convince my mother to drop the charges against his brother.

I think about how this all must have affected my parents. I am, in so many ways, like my father. He was a very quiet, humble soul. I know that this whole ordeal hurt him and my mom so very deeply. I appreciate how they both shielded me from what was going on around me. They had to be a fortress for me, when I know on the inside they must have felt as if they were crumbling to pieces. I, as a parent, imagine that that must have been what it felt like, because I would have felt the same way had it been one of my precious children.

This leads me to when I had to go to court and testify against them. What an awful day! I don't think that I have ever been so scared or so intimidated in all my life. The courtroom was quiet, dark, menacing, and dreary. Walking up to the witness stand from where I was sitting in the courtroom was not that far. Under the circumstances, it felt as if it took me an eternity to reach it. The evil looks that I got were piercing- as if somehow I was wrong for reporting them. I can still see the sinister smirk on Y's face. As I testified, they would whisper to their attorneys- all the while giving me the look of death. Do you recall the saying: "If looks could kill?" Well, let's just say I would have died that day, many times over.

After I came off the witness stand, there were others to go after me. I do recall the doctor from the hospital being called up to speak her piece. Other than her, I don't remember all the people that testified on my behalf or theirs in this case. I remember over-hearing a conversation between two female classmates that mutually knew all the individuals involved. Apparently, they had been asked to testify on the behalf of either of the defendants. They were commenting about how they weren't going to miss their finals to go to court. After I came off the witness stand, my mom told me to wait in the car. I was listening to this tape, and this song- His Truth Is Marching On, began to play. How that song ministered to me on that day! It was as if the words were being spoken directly to me- going into my ears, and from there deep down to my inner recesses. That day, that song was much like a salve that one would place on a gaping wound. It spoke life to my down trodden soul. A time later, my mother told me that when the judge gave the verdict, one of the mothers was very upset, and she came out of the courtroom ranting against me.

Shortly after our day in court, we had to go before the school board. Y showed up alone. I don't know if Z ever came because I didn't see him. I was told that the reason why Y was there alone was because his mother refused to come because he kept getting into trouble. This was the same mother who was looking for me after the verdict was given in court. It was very somber in the room on that day. The board was comprised of men and women, and I distinctly remember a blonde white woman who asked me a question that touched a nerve. It was just too much to have to tell the whole thing all over again. It was like ripping a big band-aid off a fresh injury.

After meeting with the school board, what I know is that Y and Z were not allowed to come back to the high school that we attended. I believe that they were expelled from the county. I don't know this for sure, but at this point, it's a non- factor. I don't know what the court ruling was either. My parents never spoke of the incident- any aspect of it, with me afterwards. All I knew was that it was over, and that was enough for me.

I went to Kroger with my mother one day after all of this had happened. I felt as if everyone in that store knew about what happened to me. I could feel their piercing eyes watching me. I burned with embarrassment. I told my mother about that experience, and I next found myself in a mental health office. I had a female psychologist, and she made such a big difference in my life after all of this happened. She made me feel as if I was someone special, and that it wasn't my fault that what happened to me happened to…ME. She wasn't judgmental, but she was firm. Her office was small and quaint. We would have a one- hour long session per week. She was always ready for me once I got there, and meetings proved to be beneficial and productive.

Back at school, well, it was just school. I was not very popular with Y and Z's (mutual) friends. As a matter of fact, they made a really nasty song about me and one of my classmates that I hung with. I'll never forget it. We were leaving out of the cafeteria, and were walking down the catwalk. All of a sudden, they gathered on either side of us and began chanting: "Baldhead, Muscle Head… Baldhead, Muscle Head!!!" It was happening so fast that it took a minute to just take it in. Yet, we figured out who they were referring to as baldhead (her, because she had a short haircut), and me, I was muscle head. I was muscle head because I have a big forehead. As they chanted and jeered at us, we just continued to walk to our classes. What else was there for us to do?

A year later, I got pregnant out of wedlock. While I love my daughter, this is something I am not at all proud of. My daughter is now 28 years of age. I wanted to graduate with my class, so I went to a school that would be considered an open campus. It's high school, but it is different from a traditional high school. It's like high school without all of the extra fluff- no extra curricular activities, no A, B, C, or D lunch, no high school sports, or anything like that. The sole focus is on academics. I did this because I didn't want to fall behind my class. And really, I could have... No, I SHOULD HAVE gone on ahead and graduated before the rest of my classmates back at my regular high school did. It's just that I wanted to experience walking across the stage for my diploma. Now that I look back on that, I think of what a silly girl I was to have waited. I should have just gone for it, and never looked or gone back to that school. I actually never did go back to that school after graduation. Well, I take that back. I did have to go back for my academic transcript when I enrolled in college- but that was 20 years later. I have never- and I never plan to go to any of my high school reunions, class picnics, or any activity hosted by the members of my graduating class. I lived through some pretty terrible experiences at the hands of my classmates. I have no desire to see them or to be around them again. There is no bad blood, I just don't have the desire to be around them again.

Of my experiences at the other school, I was pretty much a loner because I didn't know any of the students there. I felt alright there for a minute because no one there knew me or about what happened to me, and I felt somewhat safe- intimidated, but safe. I say I felt intimidated because I was in this new environment, where I didn't know anyone, where I quickly had to learn the ropes, where I had to get up before the crack of dawn to get to the train station (my mom would take me every morning) to catch the bus that would let my out in front of my new school, and it was all just a bit much to say the least. However, I was away from Y and Z, their friends, peers at my school, and I couldn't be hurt by them again– so I thought.

Just when I felt that I would never have to see them again, Y showed up at the train station one day when I was getting off the bus to go and catch my train. My insides sank to the lowest of sanktivity (I know it's not a word). It felt like I had melted on the inside. It was just a horrible, disgusting feeling! This happened more than once. He obviously had a great deal of time on his hands. Who in their right mind goes out of their way to make someone else's life miserable? Once, when I got off the bus that I rode to the train station from school to go to my little part time job, he got off and followed me. I stopped and confronted him, and we got into what could have become an all-out fight.

I had this math class with these girls. I remember two of them distinctly. One was a really heavy set, dark skinned, black girl. She was one of those people that you didn't bother just from the way she looked. The other girl was a fair skinned, skinny girl. The skinny girl used to ask me for paper ALL the time. And I, like an infidel, would give it to her. I didn't want to risk getting beat up for telling her no. She and her friends used to sit behind me and say nasty things about me ALL the time. This was my first encounter with an all-girl group of bullies. They didn't even know me! But, they knew Y- I found this out later on. Years later, this woman walked up to me at church.

I recognized her from school, and she said: "I remember how those girls used to say bad things about you, and how you would ignore them." After all those years, who knew anyone was watching?

While writing this book, I thought of those girls and that class. I remember walking in on them before class started one day. They were stealing answer keys from the teacher's file cabinet. I should have told on them- just like the other students that were sitting in the classroom at the time should have. This is going to sound violent, but I thought of myself standing up to the girl who was always asking for paper, and stabbing her in her hand. It's definitely too late to do something like that- not that I would. But had I, I doubt that they would've continued badgering me.

It was no coincidence that Y was showing up at the same train station where I would have to catch my train after school. I was walking with this guy who was interested in me, and Y was there at the train station as the two of us entered the station from our bus. We were having a friendly, innocent conversation, and Y walked up near us and kept saying: "Don't do it, don't do it!" The guy was oblivious to what he was talking about, but I knew what he was doing. I wasn't even interested in the guy- or anyone else for that matter, at the time. Y was like a cancer. It seemed as if he had nothing else better to do, other than trying to make my life a living hell. Maybe he needed to be seeing a psychologist more than I did.

In all honesty, it was no coincidence that Y was showing up at places where I would be, period. I remember once when me, and two of my classmates decided we would go to the mall to hang out together. I considered one of these classmates to be a 'friend'. Of the word friend, I will say that it is used loosely in our society, and I have bestowed that title upon people who didn't deserve it. She was one of them.

Anyway, these two classmates came to my house to pick me up. As we drove down the street, Y flagged the car down. He was at the house of one of our classmates that lived down the street from me. Can you believe that my 'friend' actually stopped?!?! She stopped the car, and they carried on a conversation about nothing. I sat in that back seat feeling disgraced, angry, menaced, and in utter disbelief that this was taking place. I was so outdone! It was like I was frozen. I was frozen in time with all kinds of emotions whirring about on the inside of me. Instead of sitting there in that car, I should have opened the door, got out and slammed the door closed- or better yet, left it open, and ran back up the street to my house. For me now, it would have been no problem to have done just that. But back then, I didn't possess the assertiveness to do something as simple as that. I never spoke to that girl again, afterwards. I doubt that she ever even cared.

As a kid growing up, I was extremely shy. It wasn't that my parents didn't give me the love and nurturing that I needed. My mother did so much for my siblings and I. She sacrificed so much for us, and I am extremely grateful. She was the cook, maid, chauffeur, disciplinarian- and so much more, to me, my twin brother, and my three older sisters. My dad was very big on providing for his family. He sacrificed a great deal for his family as well. I spent more time with my mother and siblings growing up than I did with my dad. He was away a lot because his job required this of him. And then when he was at home, he spent a great deal of that time resting. He drove big rigs across the country, and was on the road often. My dad and I became very close once I got older. It was then (when I got older), that I understood him better, and why some things in our lives were the way that they were.

Today, I can honestly say that my dad is still so very dear to me- I'm off on another rabbit trail. He is in Heaven now. Yet, I know that he is there cheering me on, waiting on me and the rest of the family to get there- especially my mom, his "Sweet" as he affectionately called her. My dad became my friend, in the true sense of the word, and I miss him feverishly. There is no denying that I'm his child because we share so many similarities. My dad, like me, was quiet, humble, and a voracious lover of family (there is absolutely NOTHING in this world that compares to spending time with family) to name a few of the ways in which we are alike. I said all of this to say that for the most part, my childhood was plain ol' regular. Yes, there were some crazy occurrences along the way, but for the most part, it was pretty normal. I participated in activities that required me to come out of my shell, somewhat. I sang in the choir at my church. When I was called upon to sing lead, I would cry through most of the song…sing, cry, sing, cry, sing, cry. That had to have been pretty annoying for the people that had to sit through that. I would imagine the fact that I have a pretty voice made it bearable, but God! I'm thinking that I scarred myself for life in that I do not like to hear little kids sing. I just smile and grin through it. And, don't let the child that's singing start crying like I used to… Oh, God, I just can't!

I went way, way off course there. However, I said all of that to say, I am no longer *that* girl. I am still reserved- and yes, it may take me a minute to warm up to new people. But, I am no longer anyone's door mat. Experiences- this one included, and life in general, have made me who I am today. Being sexually assaulted doesn't go away. IT NEVER GOES AWAY! This experience is something that will forever be etched in the fibers of Carla. Whenever I hear some person's story about being sexually assaulted, I can relate. Seeing a scene in a movie, or in a television show about the same, I can relate. If there are lyrics to a song, or if a sexual assault is written about in a book, I can relate. I can relate to the point that it makes me cringe!

But, I am so very sure of this one thing. Although I was indeed raped, Grace is sufficient. Don't get it twisted honey, I'm talking about Jesus. He – to the point where it makes me shake my head in awe, has ALWAYS been there. He was there when this happened to me. He was there when people didn't believe me. He was there when people talked about- and treated me worse than a dog, but didn't even know the hell that I was going through. He was there when I had to go to court. He was there when people that didn't even know me hated me. He was there when I felt alone and like I had no worth-when I felt like I didn't matter. He was there when I felt disgusting, disgusted and low. He was there when my self-esteem was lower than low, and when I became promiscuous. He was there as I gave myself away to people that didn't deserve me. He was there through it all- my good, my bad, my ugly. HE WAS THERE! And not only that, He is STILL here with me! Even though at times I didn't love Him, and I did things that I know made Him sad, He never left me. He will NEVER leave me. No matter where I go, what I do, what I say, or how I feel, GOD LOVES ME. He is in love with me. I am the apple of His eye (you are too, it's in the Bible). If I know nothing else in this life, I know that He is there. He is there/here every waking minute of my day and night- and anything in between. It takes a mighty God to hold a person up after being raped. I know this firsthand all too well. And while I acknowledge the fact that it happened, and that it did impact my life, it is not the sum total of who I am. God loves me! And for the person that is reading this book right now that feels like their world is completely out of control, GOD LOVES YOU!

This is going to sound so crazy, but I remember this one time that I went walking in my neighborhood. On this particular morning there were these men working on the road who weren't there when I left my house to go exercise. What normally would've taken me 30-45 minutes, tops, took me an extra 45 minutes! I went all out of my way to get back home because those men were there. I didn't want for them to see me! I wasn't happy about this, but I just couldn't do it. I couldn't walk where those men were working! It's not that I was afraid that they were going to try to do something to me, it's just that I feel uncomfortable in situations like that. And without fail, if I am ever somewhere where I have to walk near a group of men- be they young or old, I will quickly acknowledge their presence, and walk by with my head down pretending to be busy doing something on my phone (thank God for cell phones). Before cell phones, I would walk away quickly with my head down, or I'd try to make them think that I was preoccupied with something- like looking through my purse or something. I would do anything to quickly get out of their sight. Sounds pretty funny, huh? For me, it was and is all too real. I keep telling myself that it's not that serious (sigh).

While rape in and of itself is what it is, the experience is different for the individual. I can't tell you about someone else's experience as I can mine. It happened to me. But here I am today by the grace of God. I stand in awe of how He brought me through this horrific ordeal. The aftermath of it all could have gone in another direction- it could have very well taken me out. I could have gone mad. I could have sought out revenge. I could have done a number of things. Yet, here I stand. And I believe that because I am choosing to speak on this, there are lives that will be impacted. If you have gone through this type of horrible ordeal, and you are reading these words, you made it! You still are lovely, beautiful, and worth all that God has for you. Please know this! I remember once when I was in the middle of a vocal session with a well sought out vocalist. She said something to me that helped me move forward in writing this book. Basically, she asked me: "What is it that won't allow you to just sing (live) full out?" She went on to give me an example of the thing that made her retreat. It tripped me out that someone could sense that there was something that happened in my life that just wouldn't let me be. Not anymore.

When I started writing this book, I didn't tell any of my family members about what I was doing. Once I had gotten most of it out on paper, I read it to my husband. He was shocked! Before we had gotten married, I did mention to him that 'something happened' to me when I was a teenager. I didn't go into great detail. I wasn't trying to hide it from him or anything like that, I just didn't want to have to talk about it. Because to talk about it meant that I would, in some ways, have to re-live it. It meant that I would have to feel some of those emotions, those feelings again. It meant that I would have to deal with it, and I suppose I just didn't want to have to do that. It was- I felt, just better for me to keep it buried and go on with my life.

I don't think my husband was ready for what I told him. He had no idea the magnitude of what transpired and how it affected my life. He just kept saying: "Wow". And while he is typically quiet, yet friendly, I could sense the emotion 'soup' whirring around on the inside of him. (Yes, men most definitely have a soft side too!) After I was finished reading to him, he just sat there for a while, staring. He didn't say it quite like this, but I think that his respect for me- not as his wife, but for me as a person, went up significantly on the night that I unofficially 'unveiled' Hurt Unspoken.

One night, as we were sitting in our front room after watching a movie, I asked my husband these questions: "When I told you about what happened, how did it make you feel? What did it make you think? What state of mind were you in? How did it affect you?" This was his response:

"I mean, I felt a little angry… somewhat surprised. Even though you said I wasn't in your life at that time, I felt like something happened to a person that was a part of me. And, I mean to hear it in twenty somethin years (nervous laugh)… it was hurting me cause I felt like back then I probably could have…I don't know, done something to comfort you. I, I, I felt like being with you… I knew something went wrong within your life, I just didn't know what. Certain situations… some ways that you act… I mean you could tell that, you know, somethin went on, but I just didn't know what. And to know that that was done (long pause)…unno, it just did somethin to me. Because it's not just you, it's a lot of females that are going through the same thing… and males, too. And they are not opening up, they're just holding it.. and it's just balled up on the inside of them…and sometimes they can take their anger out on people. (long pause) But, it had to be God to bring you through this far. Not had to be, it was God that brought you through this far because some people lose their minds and commit suicide… and their self esteem is so low. And, you know, God just brought you through it… He's with you. So, I mean, even for you to write this… I just take my hats off to you. Cause there's a time and a place, and maybe this was the time for you to release it… you know, in a book cause somebody needs it. It's going to help somebody. And that's it."

After he told me this, it got pretty heavy in the room- heavy as in somber. So, to lighten things up, I changed the topic to something else.

I had the same such conversation with my mother and twin brother. One day out of the blue I told them that I was writing a book. They were both all smiles until I told them what the book was about. Both their demeanors changed. The anger on my brother's face was undeniable. The look on my mom's face was a mixture of things- anger, surprise, resolve, concern… a mixture. My brother didn't say anything much- besides a deep grunt here and there when something touched a nerve. He paced the kitchen floor, shook his head a few times, and walked out after he'd had enough.

Speaking of brothers… The love I have for my brother runs very deep. I remember when he and I had the chicken pox. He had it way worse than I did, and he looked horrible! One day, lo and behold, guess who should be walking up our street, and happened to linger a bit too long in front of our house. Yep… Y and Z. Overcome with emotions, my brother confronted them. Now, I didn't know about this until after the fact because while I was sick, I pretty much stayed in my parent's room. All I can say about this is that I have much love and respect for my brother. Not only did he look horrible with all of those chicken pox bumps on him, but he was a bit weak because we both (remember we're twins) were sick while we had the chicken pox. It sort of makes me laugh. But, can you imagine someone coming up to you looking all weird with chicken pox bumps on them? Just the sight of him alone would have made me run. This encounter would not be the last. I will say that what I was unable to do, he did. THANK YOU, brother. After all those years, you set me free.

In writing this book, I wanted to include someone else's perspective from this same experience. I reached out to a few people. However, this one person stood out. God knows why. I have so much respect for this individual because I know that this was indeed difficult to talk about. However, it allowed this person the opportunity to not only let it out, but also it shed light on those areas where healing and restoration needed to take place. During the time that I spent with this individual, my heart got very heavy. I couldn't believe what I was hearing! How someone could survive what this person went through- and not be sitting in a corner somewhere counting imaginary elephants, is totally beyond me. I cannot go into the intimate details that were shared with me in confidentiality without revealing the identity of this individual. However, here is a peek into this person's world- as it was graciously shared with me.

To be sexually violated one time is enough to shatter one's world. Imagine, if you can, this happening to a child over a period of years, by someone entrusted with their care! If we would all be honest, this happens more times than we would like to admit. This individual shared with me how their cries for help to other family members went unnoticed. People can be so busy with life that they don't see- or they choose not to see, things going on right around them. This is

MY opinion, but I would venture to say that most everybody knows someone that has been molested or raped by someone in their family. This is bad. This is a very bad thing. But even worse is the aftermath.

What really hurt was, unlike me, this person had no one to turn to for help, and was labeled fast and crazy. I had my family for support. I don't want to imagine what my life would have been like had they not been there. In actuality, I could see where the crazy part could have been true, but this individual wasn't either of those things. In my opinion, I think that the people in this person's family knew something was wrong, they just didn't know *what* was wrong. Instead of the family getting to the root of what was happening to this individual at the time, it probably was easier to just write them off. And what made this even more sickening was that the person that molested this individual molested others in front of them.

While listening to this person open up to me about their experience, I found that we were alike in a lot of ways. Promiscuity- we both experienced it after we were raped. Teen parenthood- we both became parents as teens. Self -esteem at the lowest negative number you could ever imagine, that was us. The similarities left me in awe. I mean, as this person was speaking, on the inside I was nodding in agreement at so much of what they experienced and felt. While being raped is definitely not something to celebrate, it was a relief for me to know that I was not alone. I knew that I was indeed not alone, but to have someone up close and personal speak about the same feelings and experiences was mind boggling.

After being raped, one has to pick up the pieces. Trust and believe me when I say that the pieces are many, but life does not stop. If you have walked in those shoes, you know exactly where I am coming from. When I tell you about the shame, believe me there is a lot of it. I sat in disbelief many a time and asked: "Why did this have to happen to me?" Yet, I encourage you today to live. Sure, this type of experience can suck the very life out of an individual- if allowed to.

It can dampen one's exuberance, vivacity- while at the same time cause one to question their very existence. For me, many times it made me feel as if I wasn't good enough, or pretty enough. And let's not forget the many times that I settled for less, when I should have demanded more. But, there is more. Your life doesn't have to end (figuratively or literally) just because someone chose to violate you. Don't be deceived!!! YOU are more than what you have gone through! You and I, we have come out of a fiery furnace, a burning hell, and now look! We are not defined by what we have gone through! Allow yourself to maximize your life. You have the authority to do so. NEVER, EVER look at yourself as a victim. Instead, choose to be just the opposite- victorious. And while I saved the best for last (but not the least by any means), trust in the Lord- as I do and always will. Regardless of what it may look like, His love for me and you will never fail!

Lastly, I am reminded of this scripture in the Bible:

To appoint unto them that mourn in Zion, to give unto them beauty for ashes, the oil of joy for mourning, the garment of praise for the spirit of heaviness; that they might be called trees of righteousness,

the planting of the LORD, that he might be glorified. (Isaiah 61:3)

www.ingramcontent.com/pod-product-compliance
Lightning Source LLC
Chambersburg PA
CBHW061931280526
45787CB00004B/1562